AF488272

Uphill and into the Wind
by Jeffrey Schweitzer

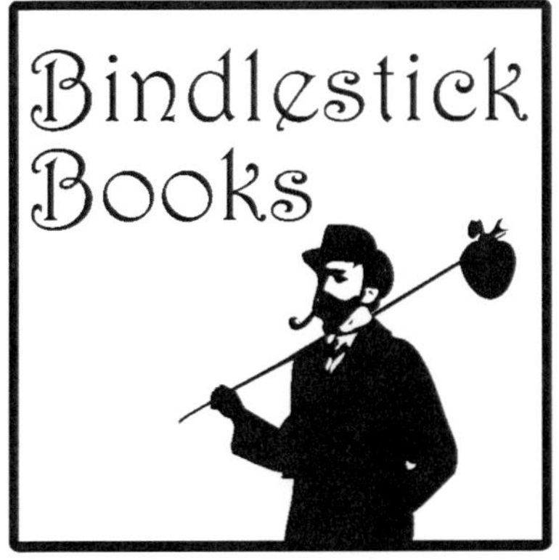

Santa Fe, New Mexico

Published by
Bindlestick Books
Santa Fe, New Mexico

First edition.
ISBN:
979-8-218-37523-2

Uphill and into the Wind

His boots felt heavy. The wind
blew ice pellets into his face,
stinging his watery eyes and
making it impossible to see
through the driving snow.

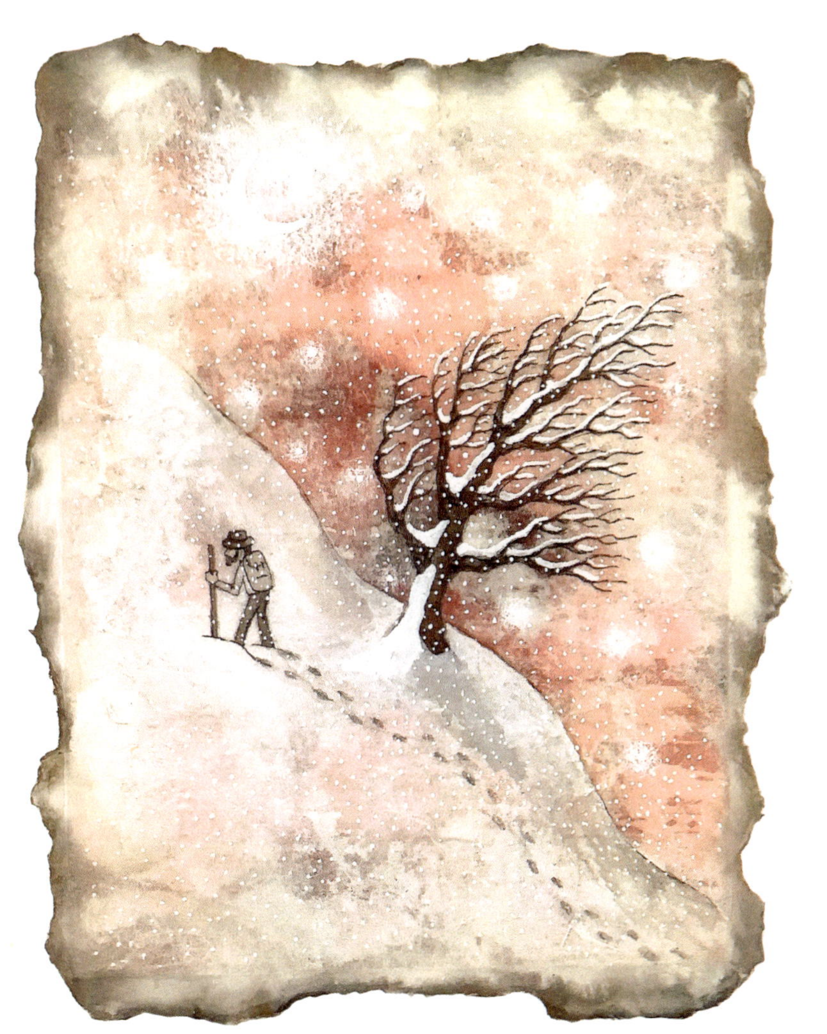

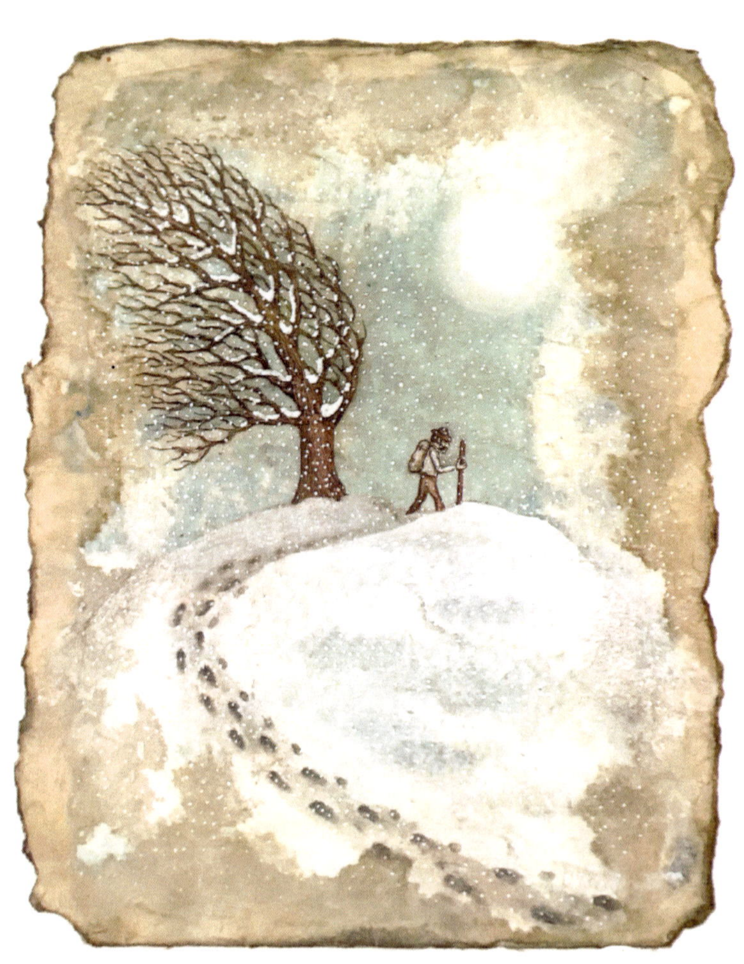

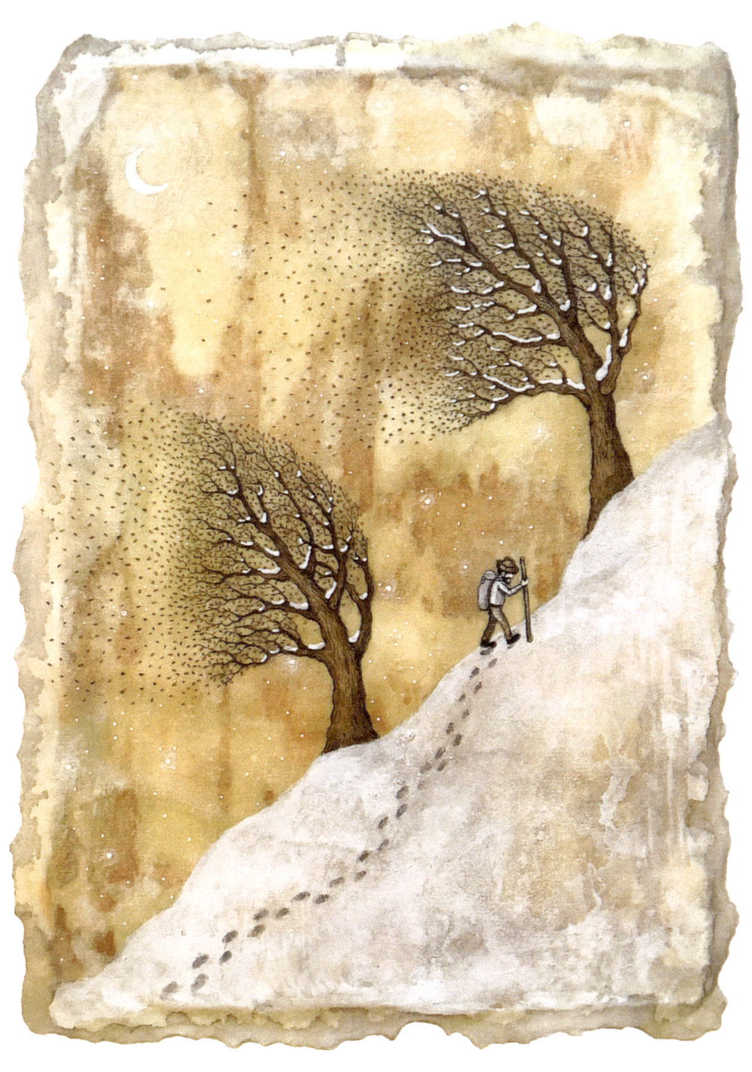

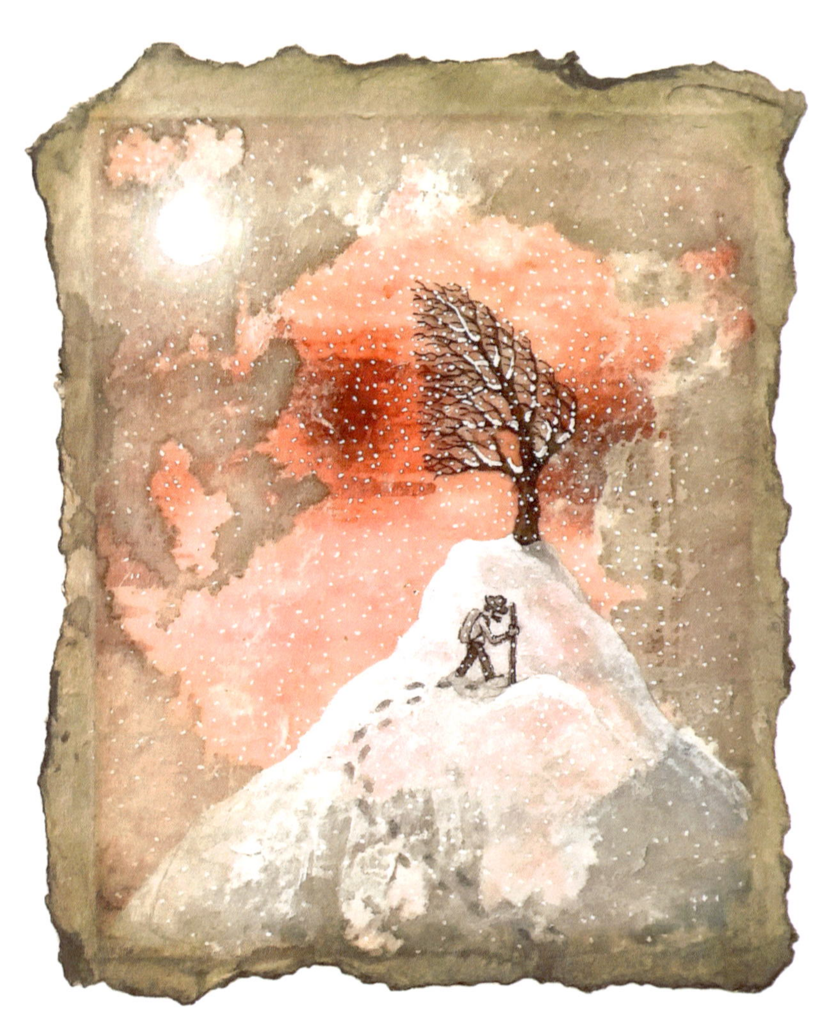

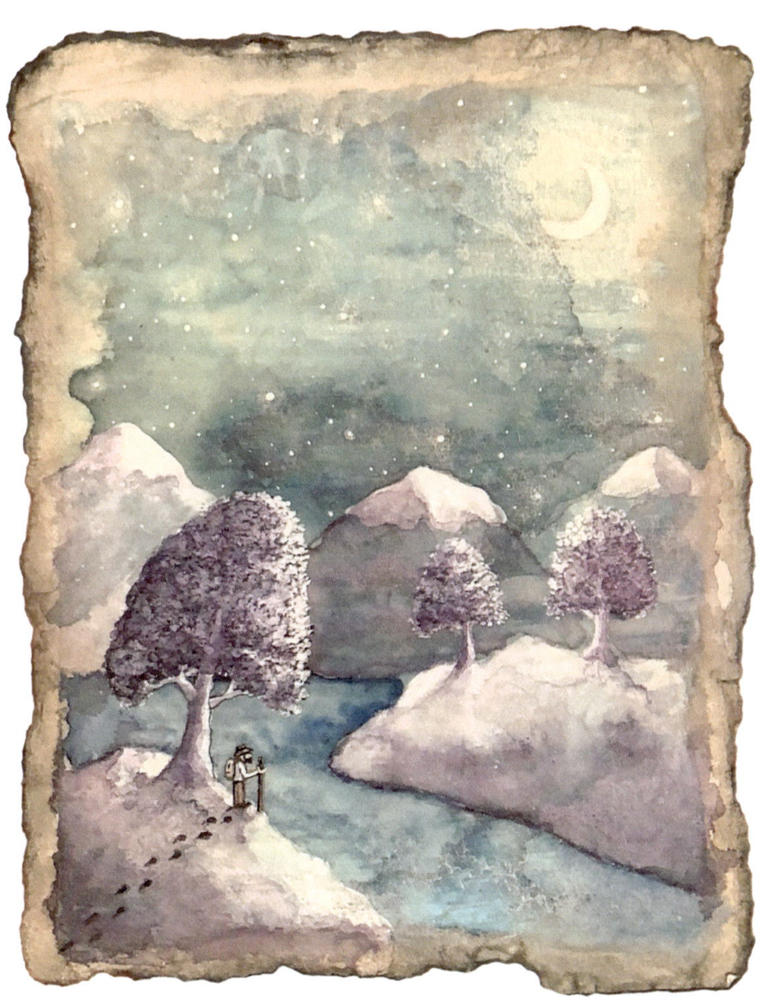

Massive storm clouds rushed overhead cresting the mountains on the freezing wind. Each relentless gust burned his lungs and took his breath away.

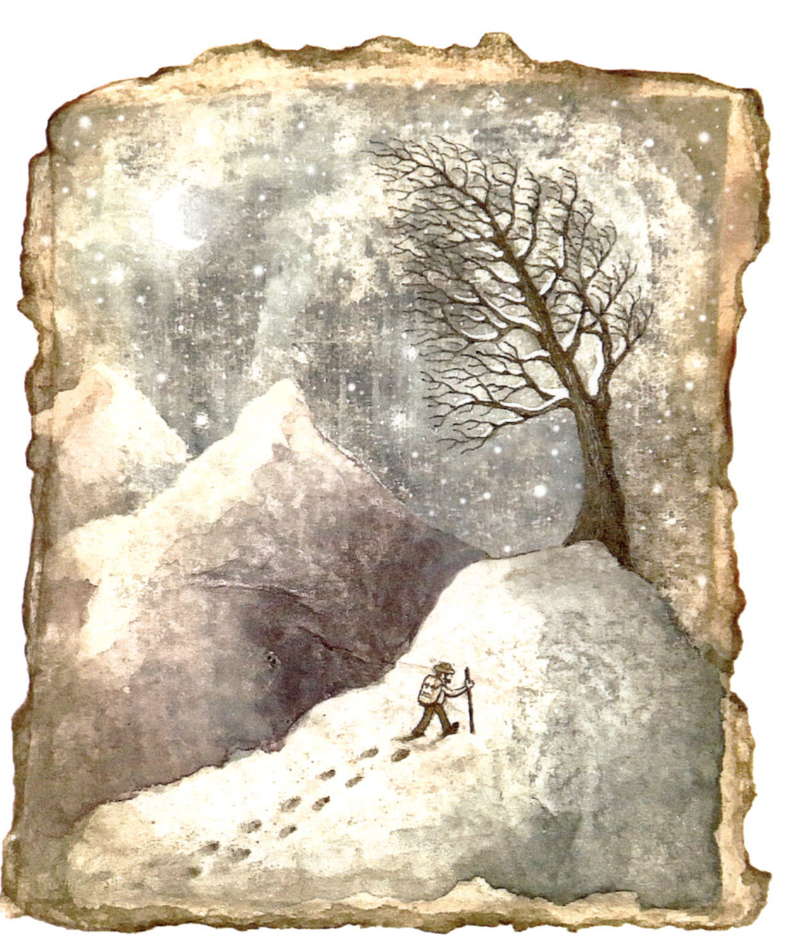

His beard had been gathering
snowflakes and condensation for
miles and was now completely
frozen over.The tips of his toes
had long since grown numb in his
soggy leather boots.

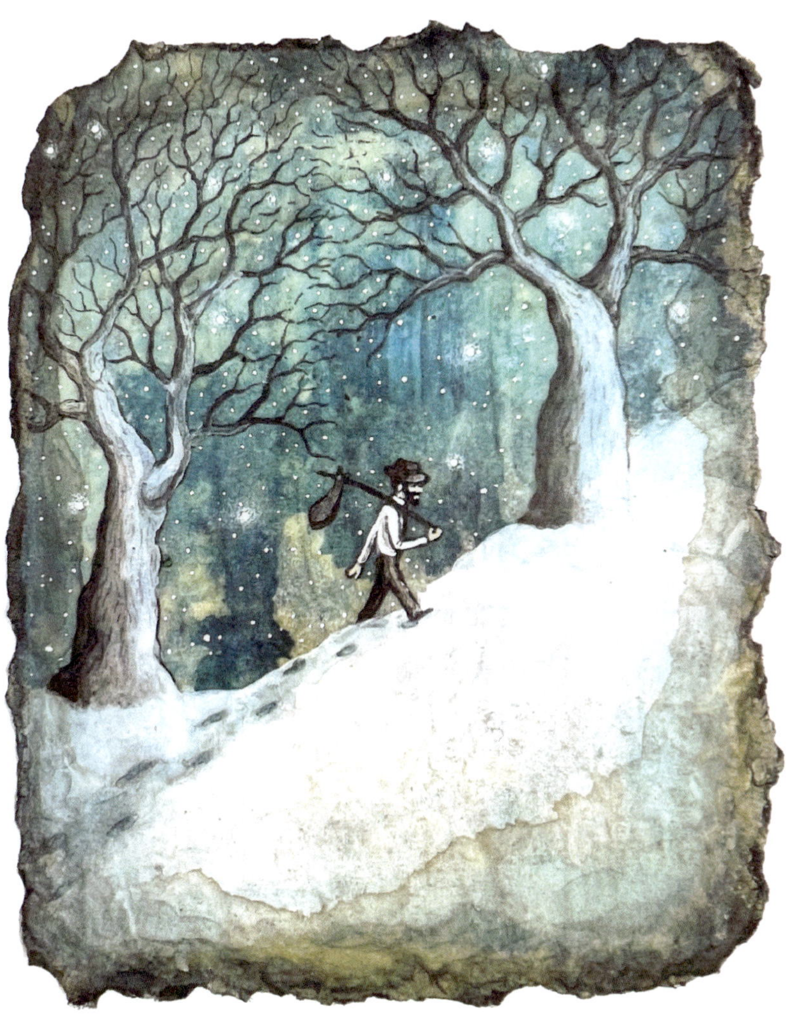

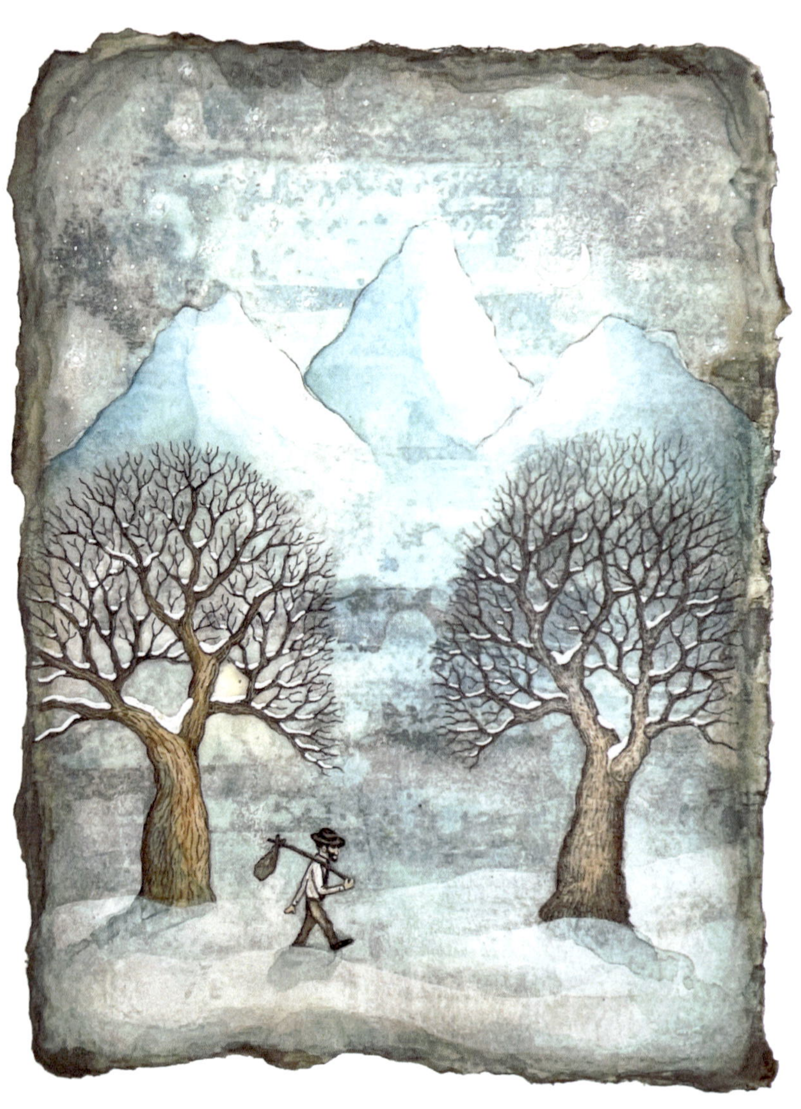

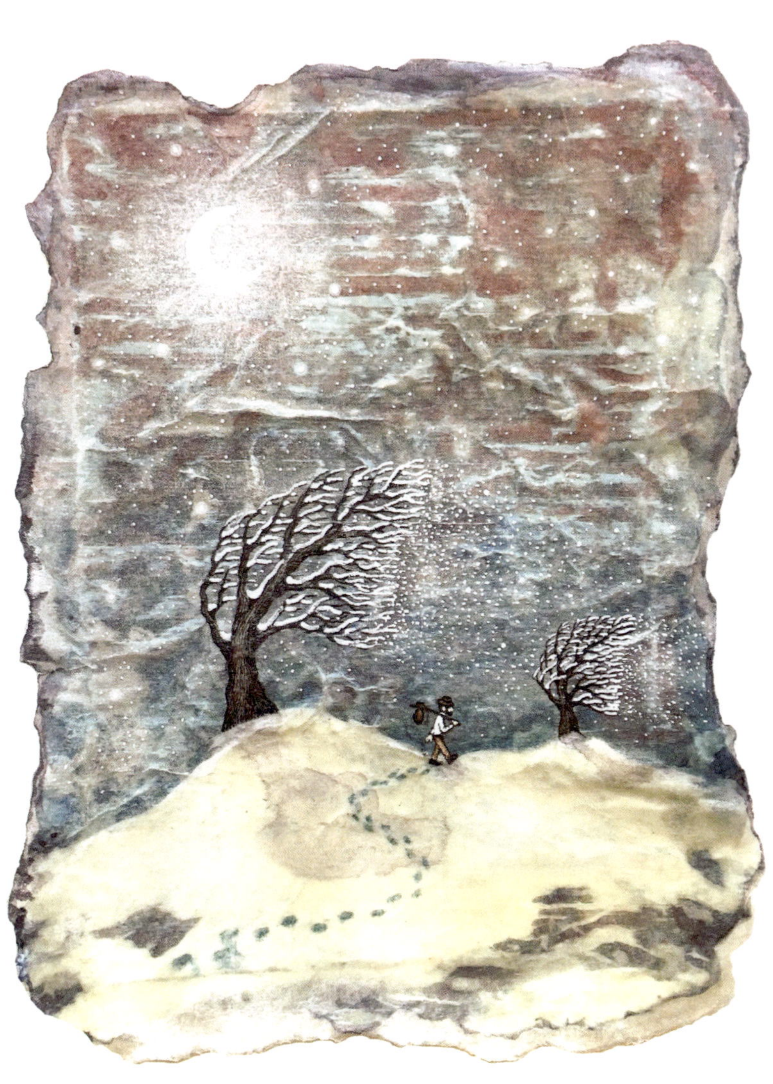

Through the blowing snow,
the faint image of his little
camper finally came into view
perched at the top of a hill.

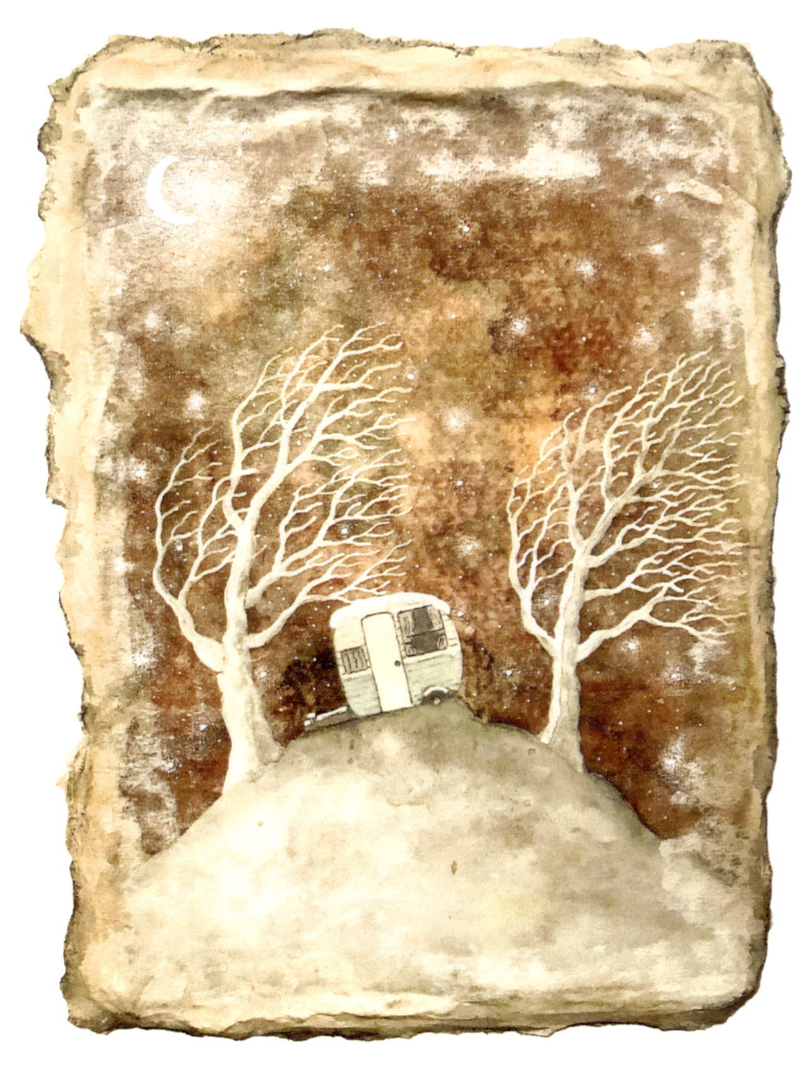

    He felt a sudden urgency to
be out of the cold and quickened
his pace through the knee-deep
snow.

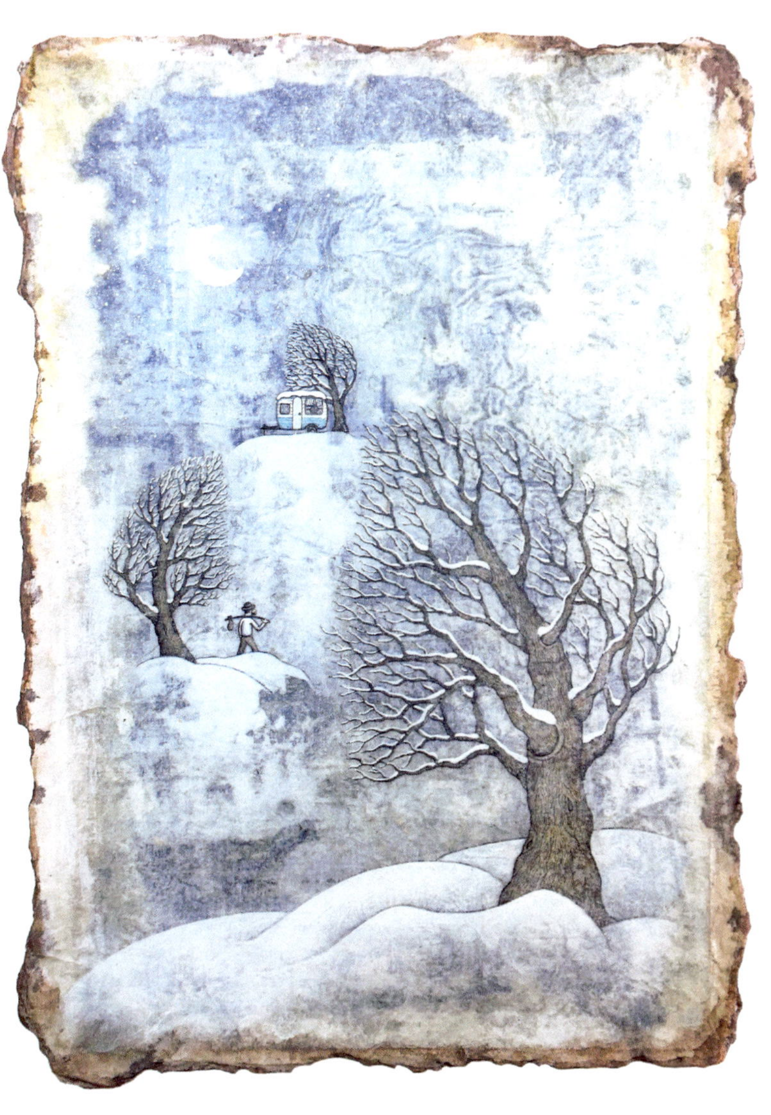

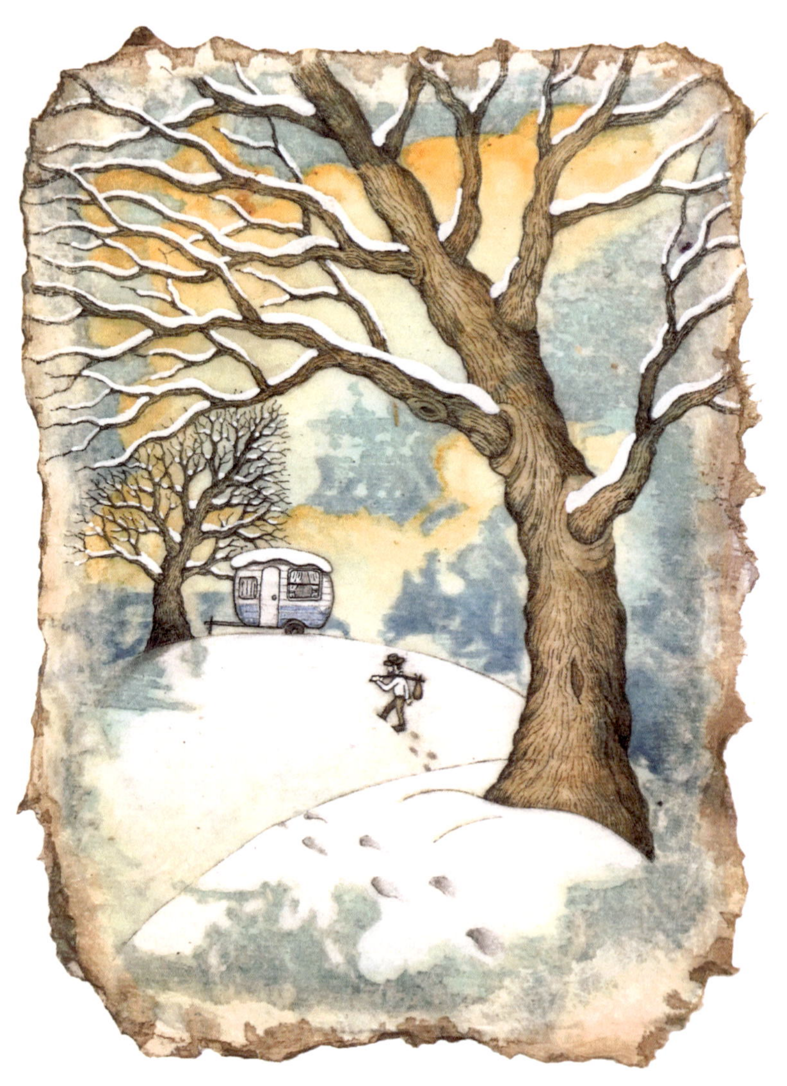

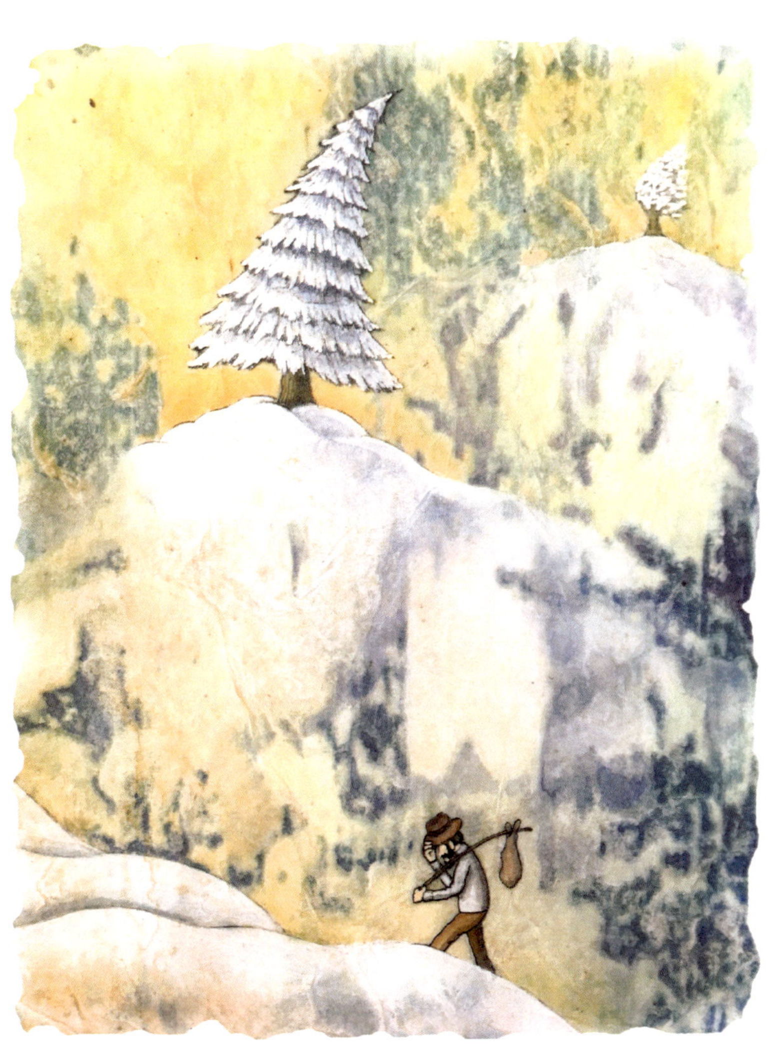

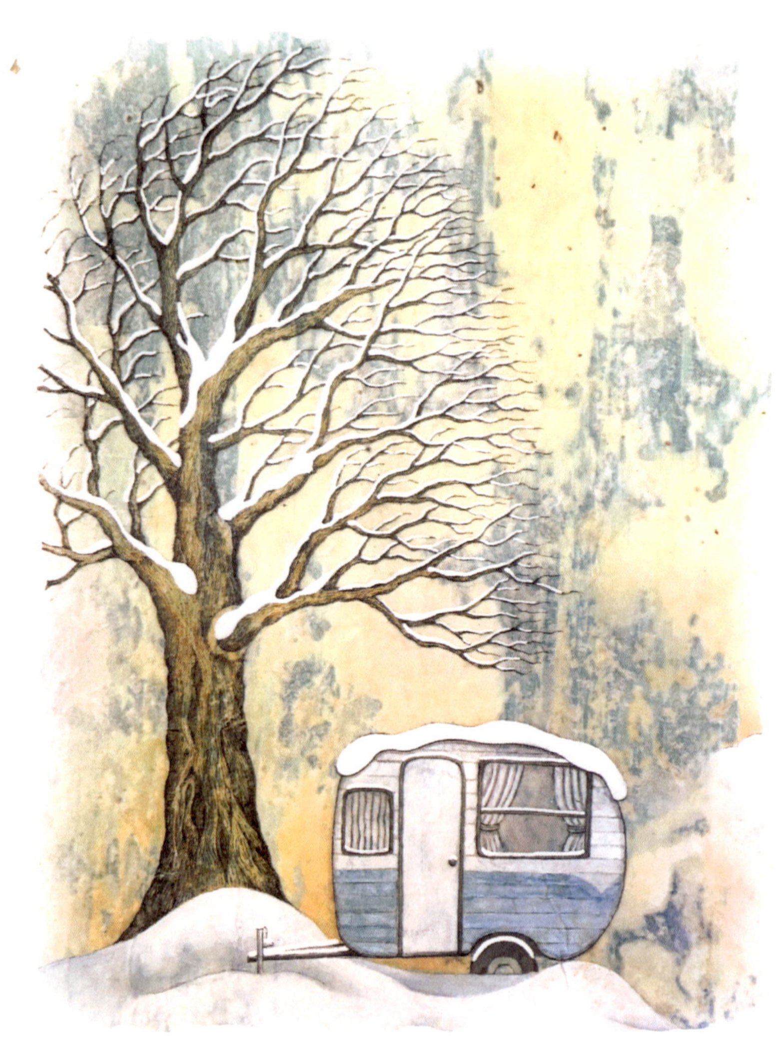

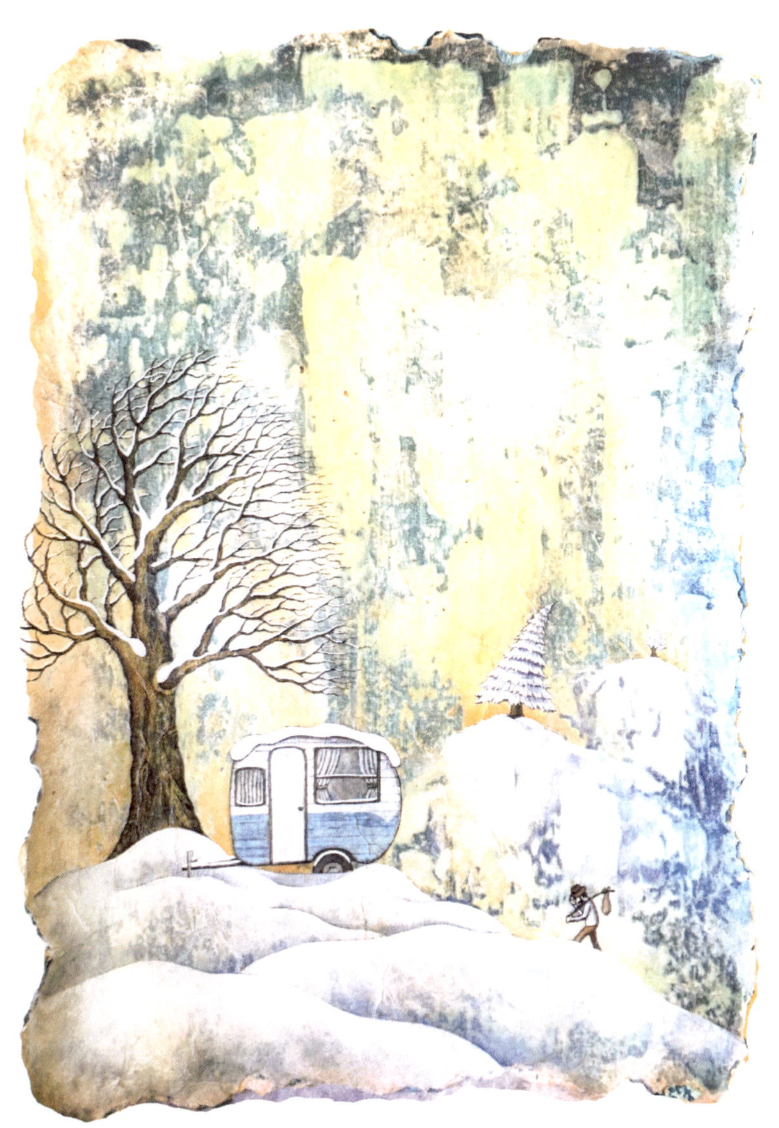

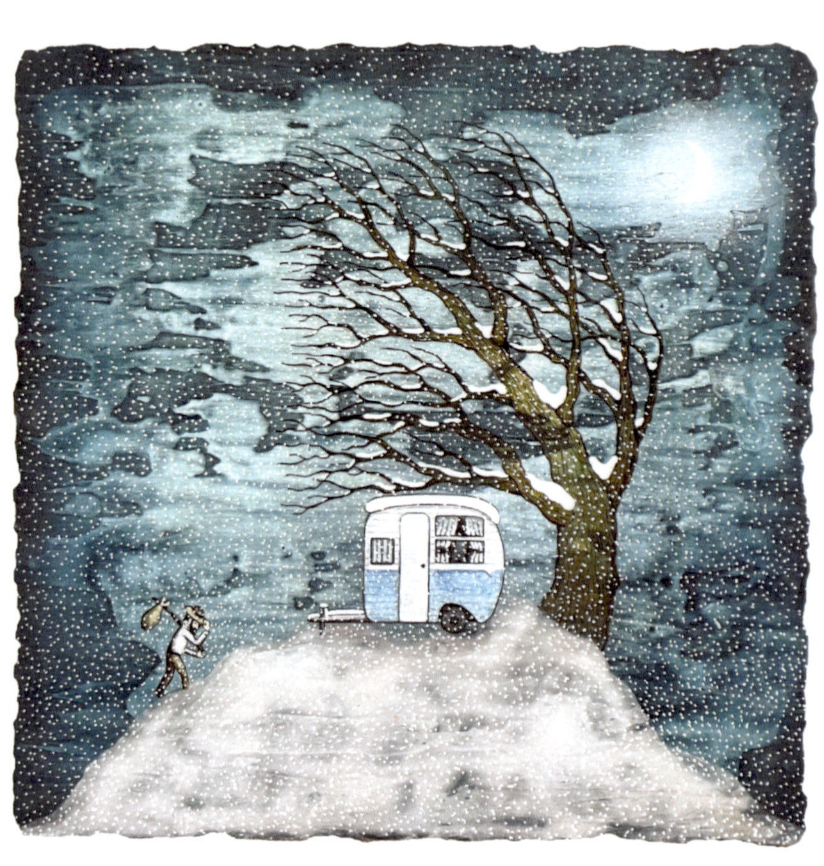

He finally made it to the
door and began rummaging through
his pockets with frozen hands.
Fumbling for his keys with
uncooperative fingers, he
promptly dropped them into the
snow.

    Cursing, he started digging
through the snow to recover
his missing key ring. Exhausted
and freezing, he pulled hard on
the door cracking away a thick
layer of ice and swung it
open with a thud. He slammed his
frozen boots against the side of
the camper to dislodge the snow
and climbed inside.

He let out a long frosty breath
and was overcome with an immediate
sense of relief. Opening the cabinets,
he dug out wool blankets and a small
propane heater. He lit the little
heater and huddled next to it trying
to get warm.

It was good to be home.

Pulling off his wet boots he
glanced at the little office in
the corner. Piles of unfinished
drawings and discarded writing
were right where he had left
them.

He shook his head. For as
long as he could remember it felt
like he was traveling uphill and
into the wind.

Perhaps now the wind was
finally at his back.

Books by Jeffrey Schweitzer.

Crows Follow Him Wherever He Goes

Uphill and into the Wind

He Lets the Stars be His Guide

Home: An Illustrated Journal

Countless Hours

The Mundane Ghost

Tales of Wizardly Whimsy

The Eccentric Gentleman

Into the Moonlight